THE PENGUIN POETS

LIVING AT THE MOVIES

Jim Carroll was born and raised in New York City. Talented at both basketball and writing, he attended Trinity High School in Manhattan on a scholarship and was an All-City basketball star—a period in his life vividly described in his widely praised *Basketball Diaries*. After a prolonged struggle with heroin addiction Carroll moved to Bolinas, California, where he was able to cure his drug addiction. While living there he became interested in the possibilities of combining the verbal sophistication of poetry with the theatrical and visceral power of rock and roll. He formed the Jim Carroll Band, and their first album release, *Catholic Boy*, has received extensive air play and public acclaim. *Living at the Movies*, first published in 1973, was his first aboveground collection of poetry. His poems have appeared in *Poetry*, *The Paris Review*, *Yale Literary Magazine*, *Big Sky*, and numerous other publications. Mr. Carroll has now returned to New York City, where he lives with his wife, Rosemary.

Living at the Movies

Jim Carroll

PENGUIN BOOKS

PENGUIN BOOKS
Published by the Penguin Group
Viking Penguin, a division of Penguin Books USA Inc.,
375 Hudson Street, New York, New York 10014, U.S.A.
Penguin Books Ltd, 27 Wrights Lane, London W8 5TZ, England
Penguin Books Australia Ltd, Ringwood, Victoria, Australia
Penguin Books Canada Ltd, 2801 John Street,
Markham, Ontario, Canada L3R 1B4
Penguin Books (N.Z.) Ltd, 182–190 Wairau Road, Auckland 10, New Zealand

Penguin Books Ltd, Registered Offices:
Harmondsworth, Middlesex, England

First published in the United States of America by
Grossman Publishers 1973
First published in Canada by
Fitzhenry and Whiteside Limited 1973
Published in Penguin Books 1981
10 9 8 7 6

LIBRARY OF CONGRESS CATALOGING IN PUBLICATION DATA
Carroll, Jim.
  Living at the movies.
  Reprint. Originally published: New York: Grossman,
1973.
  I. Title.
[PS3553.A7644L5 1981] 811'.54 81-4456
ISBN 0 14 042.290 0   AACR2

Printed in the United States of America
Set in Janson

Some of these poems have previously appeared in the following magazines,
anthologies, and pamphlets: *Poetry*, *The Paris Review*, *Angel Hair*, *The World*,
Chicago, *Best & Co.*, *Telephone*, *Stone Winds*, *The Chicago Seed*, *Penumbra*,
Adventures in Poetry, "*C*" *Magazine*, *Reindeer*, *The World Anthology* and *Another
World* (Bobbs-Merrill), *The Young American Poets #2* (Follett), *The New Poets*
(Bantam), *Organic Trains* (Penny Press), and *4 Ups & Down* (Angel Hair).

"Heroin" and "Silver Mirrors" originally published in The Yale *Lit*.
Copyright © The Yale *Lit.*, 1969. Reprinted with permission.

Contents

Living at the Movies

Blue Poles

Blue poles (well?) on the beach
in a snowless winter and

I'm too cold to ask you
why we're here but of course "we are"

where on the puzzled reef dwarves either
fish or drown in the abandoned ships

sharks dissever year-old children in search
of "young blood" Jersey acting like Europe

in an instant and lovely Mary kneeling along the quick tide
to be anxious with thoughts of bare oceans

that move as the thighs of an eventual sunlight
like bathers moving closer to their season

when again gulls perch in their lovely confusion
"alone," as now, the sand sifting through

your fingers like another's darkness. it's true,
you are always too near and I am everything

that comes moaning free and wet
through the lips of our lovely grind

The Distances

The accumulation of reefs
piling up one over the others
like thoughts of the sky increasing as the head rises
unto horizons of wet December days perforated
with idle motions of gulls . . . and our feelings.

I've been wondering about what you mean,
standing in the spray of shadows before an ocean
abandoned for winter, silent as a barque of blond hair.

and the way the clouds are bending, the way they "react"
to your position, where your hands close over your breasts
like an eyelid approving the opening of "an evening's light."

parasites attach themselves to the moss covering
your feet. blind cubans tossing pearls across the jetty,
and the sound of blood fixes our eyes on the red waves.

                              it is a shark!

and our love is that rusted bottle . . . pointing north,
the direction which we turn, conjuring up our silver knives
and spoons and erasing messages in the sand, where you wrote

"freezing in the arctic of our dreams," and I said
"yes" delaying the cold medium for a time
while you continued to "cultivate our possessions"

as the moon probably "continued" to cradle.
tan below the slant of all those wasted trees
while the scent carried us back to where we were:

dancing like the children of great diplomats
with our lean bodies draped in bedsheets and
leather flags while the orchestra made sounds

which we thought was the sky, but was only a series
of words, dying in the thick falsetto of mist.
for what can anyone create from all these things:

the fancied tilt of stars, sordid doves
burning in the hollow brick oven, oceans
which generalize tears. it is known to us

in immediate gestures, like candle drippings
on a silk floor. what are we going to do with anything?
besides pick it up gently and lay it on the breath

of still another morning. mornings which are
always remaining behind for one thing or another
shivering in our faces of pride and blooming attitude.

in the draught of winter air my horse is screaming
you are welcoming the new day with your hair leaning
against the sand. feet dive like otters in the frost

and the sudden blue seems to abandon as you leap. O
to make everything summer! soldiers move along lines
like wet motions in the violent shade's reappearance.

but what if your shadow no longer extends to my sleeping?
and your youth dissolves in my hand like a tongue, as
the squandered oceans and skies will dissolve into a single plane

(so I'll move along that plane)   unnoticed and gray
as a drift of skulls over the cool Atlantic where I am
standing now, defining you in perhaps, the only word I can.

as other words are appearing, so cunningly, on the lips
of the many strips of light. like naked bodies
stretched out along the only beach that remained,
brown and perfect below the descending of tides.

The Narrows

for Carol Kane

That is the way you are, always given
to silence. so I don't care anymore
about these green leaves in my carpet
about the death of an historical figure
about your voice.

you were thinking about a red curtain
that we might hide behind. I was
thinking about the freedom of your shadow,
last night, when this livid sky unfolded
its vault of a thousand swords and the air
we were breathing seemed our own.

I'm glad that you're able to breathe
I'm glad that you're able to distinguish me
from the lights along the thruway.
I mean don't both of us illuminate
the direction which you are taking?
and don't both weep nervously above
the moist pavement where you move.

I'd like to watch myself holding you
above the cool shore of something really vast
like a vast sea, or ocean.
and when I was through watching
I'd become someone else, seducing the heavy
waters, allowing nothing to change.
as the sands are changing and night comes
and we're not aware of all this endlessness,
which is springing up like The Moonlight Sonata
ascending from the glare of a thousand frightened moans.

August

The shower of black infants across the infected landscape . . .
birds, glaringly inhibited, as they dissolve
into the disappearance of boundaries
on a sea, filthy and darkened with bodies,
where passion rests beside the white canvas . . .

I'm lost again as I'm waking
as a wave would wake had it reached the shore:
it's like movement, something which bores us terribly,
but remains for a time to be never forgotten.

as somewhere there is a series of colors
winging their imperfect light
above your feeble reaction to it all
and spreading like blankets of trees in winter
onto the cold metal surrounding you.

while all I'm doing is gliding
toward some future, composed of plants and stones,
that passionate oasis, aware of fire dragged
through the mist of all those other possibilities:
moonlike emotion over this flat harbor,
moon exhausted across your embarrassed hand
where I finger this light eventually
of the rainbow you have constructed
like numbers along the map of some great thruway
thoughtlessly arranging some final confusion:

in the morning up early to look for you.

Traffic

I was a young pilot in World War I, remember?
do you know the feeling of an airplane crashing the water's edge?

we've just traveled 600 miles, and the only person
we know is sleeping under the wet almond tree.

there is nothing left but this meadow which smells of blood,
an infant has escaped from the orphanage long enough to be crushed
various birds admit their secret hate for us
and the canoe makes way through the cave for the abandoned North.

these fields open gently . . .
and the soft flowers are radiated within.

Styro

We'll stay until ice begins
over the driftwood

do you,
a girl from kansas,
imagine the invisible changes
in front of you?
and water wed constantly to sand
by foam beads . . .

pure directions of the sun
level the ocean
in your cupped palms

gulls play in their crude reflection
a tanker passes to split Europe

there is no other place that allows us
to understand so little, you see . . .

all those minds shot down by a cloud's emptiness

and our youth clung tightly
in white dunes . . .
they'll see us dreaming there
clumsy in these plaid blankets
at night.   it's

like watching wind push seaflowers
straight across your eyelids
or the sun melt them, either way

they'll be gone eventually
and new forms will take shape
and grow, even before we're gone

this will happen.

Morning

1.

Today the room is filled with tomorrows   the machines failed
continuously   they got undressed   the tools being electric
three elbows cast in light   the sculptor's dreams spilling like
gray marbles   one over the other shadow   speed fell along the
wooden desk   downstairs the rape continued   a boy screaming
for his cat   windows crawled with vines   you are discovering
your eyes carved in enamel   over the dictionary flew last slabs
of plaster   what is that you needed from the clinic?

we could have afforded more than this   one does not pay for
leaf, sooty tear, membrane, or rare tints of ember   and receiving
is acting fatal, I guess   clocks alone maintained their retarded
movement   or darkness maybe   now I can think of her   lost
in the fine spray of a stream beside a dog's leg   you wanted so
much more   hour hands folding over like green sandwiches
"this earth is slowly . . ."   a nail tore apart the fruit later we
moved upstate and lit fires on the lawn   China provided lan-
terns   underwater the squid evidently didn't reach the road
everybody joined us at the bar   it is a holyday in France   a
speaker remains on the stout platform.

2.

proper authorities served us with precautions   the light top-
pled the aluminum support   "first the basement . . . then the
border patrol" but pretending one was another was a nauseous
feeling   I want eyes in your left arm   I'm not easy to please
didn't I tell you?   rivers are beginning to evaporate the chalk
figures the children made   this day seems destined to look like
salt in the theater alcohol flew   from the mezzanine   the final
results came uptown   in the warehouse the discussed invento-
ry: a red garter belt   coffee   17 thighs   and the tainted
strainer   she incorporates the ideas   pearls are dipped in Au-
gust   everything was shuffled along the steaming tennis court
even the water had finished acting sly.

the other actresses ground flowers on the indian's skull   your
breast a brick white and longer than the extremely cold bam-
boo   "I limit myself, yes," said the dog,   "but I'm happy,"   I
seemingly can't take any suspense   all these abandoned slums
the sabres attached themselves to the gasoline foam   which
was only a measuring stick   which was only feet and yards
giving a geometry to our feelings   in stepped the victim   out
ran the prison walls freckled in some sections with brown ink.

the white chair suspended dignity   soon the impeccable aunt
who came to visit   her mouth had been jammed with leather
mechanically an oven boiling scotch tape   the dust opened to
our hands like blue roses   fire engines avoided the yellow
detour   "I must laugh if I tell you this, but I only feel like a
torpedo now and then"   barb wire hawks surrounded the
barn   12 year-olds peddled downhill   right into the thorn
berries   his ankle swollen by the pace "we won the pennant
at last!"   later he returned in a bread truck all were dancing
in the ochre garden   the negro maid put in the token   her
husband praying like dice   the old cornices   clarinets were
mistaken for red lightbulbs   there is never anything remain-
ing for ransom money though, was there?   we always desire
the excess: abundance of tri-colored petals   texture of the
funneled wind   tinseled vapors dripped like feathers into the
aquarium   our ring of meteors collapsed   soon the amusement
park was destroyed   desire is clipped like angel hair   falling
everything   even the dark green landscape   tree by tree   for-
est by forest.

Next Door

Today a hockey player died in
my dreams the lady takes her vows
I'm a nun the hallway is ringing with
drunks a cat sleeps on the roof
black as six years of snow that's
Tom my brother age one more than
me I'm 18 and you? you're lovely
thinking about my future the poems
laid waste in my head the stone
comes through the window like an
owl breaks everything into replace-
able parts like the poems laid waste
in my head the phone is trying to
tell us something my sky is a
friendly dome I'm so near to
everything yes H. Read making
coffee out of mold the kitchen
is burning basketballs "roll"
carrying all our energy of youth
warm gyms on wet Sundays the
pain of heat on concrete are you
trying to escape like evening?

A. Pope letting *his* amber fall
on *my* thorns O death of shepherd
me! O half-dressed shades of
voluptuous gold this whole night
while I love you as I watch you
where you are sleeping still perfectly warm

The Green Bus

What time is it in your bedroom?
the streets are becoming the red sea
        flushed through the white forest
where Gauguin was last seen saying goodbye

     despair in America (and Europe) oh!
we are here on 53rd and 6th watching steel
               change to ivy   taxi's
sexy dreams pierce your left ventricle
          your left wrist is broken,

but the time!
        a wristwatch quickly sliding down the facade
it is 5 a.m.
     time to anticipate
        we anticipate
what we anticipate is a vision:
foresight among the fathers slowly withdrawing from the legion
seeking the insoluble answer of the waves   I mean the streets
do you realize "I hate you"   now you sneeze

(it isn't easy talking to you
        through the brick genitals you're holding,
and I tremble without boots or wings,
sitting exhausted upon the serpent's breath

a fan moves in the sky   you are a very happy person
it drips the sordid blood
        it stops . . .   the heat!
    it is 5 a.m. in the Warwick Coffee Shop
it is 5:10 in N.Y.
           I am in N.Y. . . .

"no more fiesta along Houston St." she remarked
    "smear the river with doves and praise
            the departing feathers"

(I don't know from your bedroom what you're thinking,
      said the "person"   do you want to take in a movie,
and go home after and fuck maybe?

            you are warm today and the climate
                    is happy and welcomed

shall we walk, then, to the park?
      near the fountain?
           shall we sit in the grass?

The Loft

So I move through the black doorway
to be turned headon into light
and the phone was desperate
to speak to tell you something
in the next room she pants like 8th St.
the drawers swept the powdery substance
through the green shaft and
it was Thursday because of your breath.

(the effulgence of your sway
and total landscape of clockblood

I have produced the ransom once more
and the third of five angels is set free
to resurrect / and be buried again

so that I hardly remember the
composed landscape and waters
the rose violin the basketball teams

I was happy as you were about the whole thing
I saved for months . . . the calendar is crushed
"put on your rifle," they told her, "death
is only white by nature"
evening is so vain lately
like your lips geometry.

should anything have come to this, love?
take the yellow typewriter,
it's winter   I'm so glad
and the wind is pushing like pinecones
against the angel's dying sperm.

In the Valley

Everyone's eyes broke
when they woke earlier than usual
today
to the hum of the winter moth

mostly we fixed windows after that
it was worse than when we tried
to make the ceiling flat
again
after the heavy rains last Spring

after rainy lunch at the fountain
we assembled ladders and attacked
the snowbirds that gather along the wires
when the sun's half cut by the mountain.

flowers, eagles and children
twice the size of other children,
demagnetizing skybulbs,
the factory . . . and retired celebs
are what we are proudest of here . . .

Tonight we play with needles
in our ponchos, wavering,
it is cool, it is clear . . .
it is wholesome in this valley

The Burning of Bustin's Island

As you enter the room a door knob
possibly hundreds of years older than your oldest relative . . .

work has suddenly offered its hand to me like a boxer
and noises round and for the most part fake have crept . . .

on the lawn a green bike leans its broken fender
against the pinecone, a boy waves then throws the ball into . . .

light producing a condition between which nothing
grows and horses spring up like a field must . . .

sooner or later a bench near the eastern cove will
dump its clients overboard and they will have mud . . .

at last a breath of fresh sea water, spray reoccurring
like a day a dream close to the shadow of speed . . .

split by light and dark.

Love Rockets

Wet leaves along the threshold of the mid-day
and I'm off to rescue the sky from its assassins
jogging and screaming and launching my clean mortars

into the March obscene air . . . the enemy.

I suppose I'd rather be sitting in Samoa now
sipping a quart of Orange Julius and being fanned
by Joey Heatherton in black tights and white glossy lipstick.
but I'm not. I'm here. and I have something to say,

as well as something to take care of.

And that something is probably more important than
you realize. I like the sky (don't you) its warmth, its friendliness,
I'm not going to let all this fucking soot taint that terrific blue.

battle the filthy airs with your mortars and your prayers.

you'll soon be overcome with lovely sensations of the sky.
you'll be thinking of me as this happens.

The Other Garden

Now I want to return
for your fingers are like a thousand silk ponies
mounted along the icy miles.
    "the exquisite grasp of this land we do love
                    and awake to on Sundays"
but what is time since you've discovered what it means?
we are dying now like frozen breath,
and our hands are extended far out into the hordes of light.

now I want to return because we were
always there anyway weren't we
when the telephone wire stretched
across the farther valley, supporting
the tiny snow birds, the day the ranger
arrived and presented us desire. the shallow
rocks swallowing the frog, three of us
pulling our fingers away from the frightened moss
"home" you might have called it,
it was evening continuously, or at least not morning
the winds of lice sweeping us over some future nation
(I wasn't built by any process other than
                    the poem itself, thus I am ashamed
                    of making distinctions like this.)
distance falling over the wet colors
like mauve tongues, the fowl was taken
behind the barn . . . last week . . . your eyes
are like squashed hands . . . I can't stand it . . .
it's snowing green handbags . . . I'm falling . . . dark reeds
are lost upon the lips . . . I adore you.
now I've lost the key again. through the window
came the split morning glories, as if
they knew about legs. there were so many more
incidents which you never really explained:
of the field, the magnet tugging at the appliance,
the grapefruit smile and of course
                    the bed of sperm.

but I never let myself be taken in
by that deep, flowing what? for I always
remembered you that way, like a clock
leaning on a breast; like a mouse.

Heroin

Sat for three days in a white room
a tiny truck of white flowers
was driving through the empty window
to warn off your neighbors
and their miniature flashlights.

by afternoon
across the lake
a blind sportsman had lost his canoe.
he swam
by evening
toward the paper cup
of my hand.

At dawn,
clever housewives tow my Dutch kitchen
across the lawn.
and in the mail a tiny circus
filled with ponies
had arrived.

You,
a woman with feathers
have come so often lately
under my rubber veranda
that I'm tearing apart all those tactless warnings
embroidered across your forehead.

Marc,
I'm beginning to see those sounds
that I never even thought
I would hear.

Over there a door is knocking
for example
with someone you hate.

and here I beg another to possess somehow
the warmth of these wooden eyes

so beside me
a lightbulb is revolving
wall to wall,
a reminder of the great sun
which had otherwise completely collapsed
down to the sore toe of the white universe.

its chalky light
rings
like a garden of tiny vegetables
to gather the quiet of these wet feelings
together

once again

like the sound of a watch
on your cold white wrist
which is reaching for a particular moment
to reoccur . . .

which is here . . . now.

Poem

We are very much a part of the boredom
of early Spring of planning the days shopping
of riding down Fifth on a bus terrified by easter.

but here we are anyway, surviving like a wet street in August
and keeping our eye on each other as we "do it," well,
you go west on 8th St. and buy something mystical to wear
and I'll simply tuck my hands into my corduroy pockets
and whistle over to Carter's for the poster he promised me.

I like the idea of leaving you for a while
knowing I'll see you again while boring books
W. H. Auden, and movie schedules sustain my isolation
and all the while my mind's leaning on you like my body
would like to lean on you below some statue in Central Park
in the lion house at the Bronx Zoo on a bed in Forest Hills on a bus.

I reach 3rd avenue, its blue traffic, I knew I would sooner
or later and there you are in the wind of Astor Place reading
a book and breathing in the air every few seconds
                            you're so consistent.

Isn't the day so confetti-like? pieces of warm flesh tickling
my face on St. Mark's Place and my heart pounding like a negro
                                                        youth
while depth is approaching everywhere in the sky and in your touch.

Birthday Poem

1.

3 hours into the afternoon of March 9th
and the morning is still lingering like a cloud
reflected onto a building on 53rd St.
where I am.
the streets are much too involved   (with what?)
much too wet too   (with rain)
though I don't mind the rain
only the wet streets and
Ron Padgett might or might not agree with that,
but we're having breakfast together nonetheless.

2.

Ron Padgett is holding two birthday gifts
which come in the form of two books
one being the works of an Italian poet
whose name I quite honestly don't remember
the other book is some selected works of Zeno
whose thoughts on motion I find very entertaining
though they're not very useful   (for me at least)
the person about to receive these gifts
is George Schneeman, who is lucky enough
to be having a birthday today.
it's also lucky for Ron that this is true
because wouldn't it be embarrassing
giving George gifts today
if his birthday were, say, a week ago
or a week ahead.

3.

but everything has worked out fine,
not like the weather
which is as dark as a laundry closet
in a very "cheap" hotel
"on a day like this I feel like I'm indoors,"

says Ron walking
to the subway of France (?) well
it seems like France
for a time boarding the first car
and watching teenagers giving up
their seats to pregnant women
or those mutilated in the war and
anyone wearing one of those
tiny red pins   (get up Ron)

4.

it's still gray and wet almost pink
as we reach E. 14th and shake hands goodbye
like someone else I'm reminded of now
writing this poem.
and I catch the bus to Ted Berrigan's
who never showed up anywhere,
least of all here on E.14th St.
right below Larry Rivers' studio
which is the route my bus is taking.

5.

I hope that George enjoys the gifts
that Ron will give him tonight.
I guess if I saw George now I'd
like to be holding something really valuable
to give him also.
but as things go (on E.2nd St.) all I'm
holding is a 25¢ orange drink
and what would George Schneeman want that for
well I was thinking of something more valuable anyway,
like a Mercedes Benz or a great feeling
like I have right now,
just realizing that someone you know was born today.

Seltzer

1.

Here is my room, smiling like a forest
of navels   yet, in secret,
                              so sad and filthy.

2.

breathe deep enough and we are possessed.
breathe again and we will be gone.

3.

the best thing about today
is the idea of tomorrow.
                    we will go on a picnic.

4.

who can argue with 6000 swallows
flying from a single cloud,
                         like joy.

5.

when we die we might see the Virgin Mary
sitting before the father, the son, and the Holy Ghost

right now I'll settle for you
with your bra unhooked   (under a tree)
on the Staten Island ferry.

Living at the Movies

for Ted Berrigan

1.

There is a stadium beside my window
                    filled with winter
and it is afternoon   alight and barrowing my tears
so by day the message arrives   and by night
I am writing.   marvelous joy of "being sure"
pain sweats the hunger upon its teeth   the days
of white miracles break through   sun over the Harlem River
2:23   the fields are gone, moist and trembling.
she plumbs to the purple earth
                    light rising into her features.

2.

So months of cool flowers close in these arms:
decay with their green obscenity.   denial of everything
in an instant!
        (how strange to be gone)   (to be sure)
like René Magritte devouring an apple
                            (or two)
that's my language,   divisions of words I know:
                    "love:sky"

3.

It is afternoon   a sailor is crying above the waterfall
so we bend our heads and pretend to be praying   yes,
I have abandoned the starlets and their mothers
                    and trees are growing on your avenue,
teeth sweating the hungry pain   takes her away in the form
of death or love and
        O to ease the stupidity of my dreams
in the orange wet of loneliness at midnight
                        where in abandoned towers
a young shepherd is sleeping
(and you know it)

4.

Into a swamp this heart is flying
like Mayakovsky's last breath
     death full of gravity and Frank O'Hara
I have abandoned . . . and I am crying   it is midnight
and she knows it. marvelous joy of miracles breaks through
I lick the sweat upon the hungry pain.
I wonder if she's ever hungry
         I wonder if she's thinking of pain
it is midnight   she plumbs to the purple day
and O to think of her that way.

5.

light rising into her features where
into a swamp this poem is flying the
starlets and their mothers are gone
         they plumb to the earth extinct
so all that's left is she   taken away in the form
            of death or love.
the blue day breaks through in miracles.
the miracles are gone.   (how strange to be gone)
like Mayakovsky's last breath.   René Magritte
devouring the earth's plumb   light rising into
our features the dark obscenity and O to think
of her that way   it is morning and she is crying
the trees on her avenue are flying   wet orange loneliness
of her stupid dreams disappearing
     into a swamp where rise these purple days.

Your Daughter

In this month arks
deposit supplies along the shore

sand drenched . . .

    the river   suddenly the sea

now lifted up beside your heels
which warns of light in the eye of what you are holding.

your passion:

        a white mountain disappearing in the mirror.

to awake to the joy of your cold abstraction . . .
as horses returning somewhere her tight grasping the sea and air.

Fragment: Little N.Y. Ode

I sleep on a tar roof

      scream my songs
             into lazy floods of stars . . .

a white powder paddles through blood and heart

                                     and

the sounds return

                pure and easy . . .

this city is on my side

Cough Syrup

There's a hockey puck in front of the air on the window sill

I see this contraption as infinity . . .

though it's covered with dust . . .
I want to touch it

but I'll have to wash my hands
because I got leukemia in N.Y. this afternoon

One Flight Up

The people upstairs are cold
the girl with the full-sized German shepherd
and the boy who sleeps with her
are rapping against the radiator
with a spoon, it sounds like.

their message must carry down
one more flight to the janitor
whose business this is.

I can hear the steam
already beginning
in the pipe beside me

and soon the pressure will carry it higher
and the entire building will be warmer,
thanks to them, to sleep in.

How Relaxed

The way a man sits
all day on a manhole cover
contemplating a rubber stamp,

until a volkswagen brushes by
on your arm
and you're left with an idea
of, say, a man washing windows

who would rather be teeing off
somewhere in Rye, N.Y.

green

For Ezra Pound

I watched the secret
head of Mussolini
bobbing like a wet balloon
behind a strolling bush
in Vermont's sticky dawn

I made a fist . . . but dig:

a healthy cricket sat
and noticed this too
and he immediately ex-
pelled a harmless goo

        over the thought

of Mussolini   (I swear)
running from me
to avoid getting snagged
and punished for his million atrocities.

The Blue Pill

I took the blue pill this morning

I got new angles on the trees across the driveway

Timmie the bear
does his little roll on the rug

and at night
a sound gathers the tiny ambulances
from their homes

it is distant and hollow

a little like the sound
of a perfectly tuned ocarina

Blood Bridge

White ship disappears
into wave machine . . . this morning

your eyes got shot with
secret chains

that pill armies eventually
set free.

you queens so often, in fact,
open my graceful anxieties

like soft horses through toy deserts . . .

I love this mansion
though it's too many windows

to open halfway each morning
to close halfway each night

Poem on My Son's Birthday

At dawn
on the window sill
it's watery trees it's light
it's just hanging there waiting

poetry

I want to walk   you can come or
you can sleep or
you can dream of walking someplace better

and that still means we're not together

    except today
    one more day   (you were born)

It's a communion
you can hardly see
a kind of reunion   just a little one

you and me.

Crossed Wires

In 1943 the Germans sent me postcards.

I laughed heartily.

now each new day heats my cavity
I hear light scratches in the walls
drink orange pekoe tea
and weep.

I've learned nothing
I've just watched children hang across the back yard
like glittering crossed wires
exposed with silver air.

Leaving N.Y.C.

I spent a wonderful day
with two real Dutch ladies
in postcard outfits
in front of a pleasant house
with a brown tiled roof
and a brick facade with blue windows
not thinking about poetry, music,
movies, paintings, priests or nuns,

or you.

A Fragment

When I see a rabbit
crushed by a moving van
I have dreams of maniac computers
miscalculating serious items
pertinent to our lives.

Vacation

White leaf trailing the water light

and of course the stones are too much for these waters
so if one sinks
colors fall upward and blind us.
you are surrounding "the edge" now
stockings shake some craggy wetness into my ear
where I hear strange sounds.

I guess it is too often:
your fingers slipping unto my eye
high in those mountains
like a hunter.
birds thrown upward
like a hand near a lake
and your face is held before the sun
as a letter attached to a tree.

that you
yellow as the June feathered air
should hike to my window this morning
and deliver this shape
like a heart lost
within a field no one can locate.
a calf's heart probably.

I don't know about meadows
once I rode a sled
through an entire month of summer
and never landed anywhere
bees touched me and went away
I was grateful for that but now
a tree has landed across my skinny chest.

the most complex dream
ends near a swamp . . .

and horses move inverted on the gas station ceiling
I would drop like a cocoon from space
but I don't understand the very atmosphere.
my legs curl in the fog.

now you are lying on your back letting
birds open your thighs and
like a gesture I fling these loose eyes
into the steam of August.
bricks dissolve around the riverbank.

it is what keeps me from you.

A Short Reminder

They've tricked you, these boundaries
the way each stares back to the next
hoping the change might occur.

but the organ started up again
as the hand tightened the grip
on the knob of the door
the way you only guessed it should be.

up until now the way a star
greets you so openly, you forgot
for a moment that it meant nothing afterall
thought tonight it was all you had ever hoped.

                              and you were right.

because the people are all gathered
along the cliffs . . . hung like breath
their hearts are like the pets
of some terribly dreary penthouse
as clouds descend to protect their dreams

then the trees pointed off . . . over there
where the man stands hunched over the slope
who was he? and what did he want?
becoming a part of it ? that same "it"?
only more useless now, intricate as a nipple,
though so easily realized even along
the busiest streets of daylight, the spirit
that leaves you tangled in some later hour

                              which is here

where the paintings drop to the floor in rows
because you do not care to think about them again
now that you have developed this power to forget about pain
innocent, of course, but hands shaking nonetheless

you sit down in a restaurant and a glass
breaks on the heel of your shoe . . . people turn . . .
outside the window a pathway of heat guided from star to tree
breathless at first . . . but where is the solution?
and why the tree so alike each of the others, so that

when space comes into the formula the only thing
you concede is that you're "in it"

                                    guided by another like you

Gliding

Devereaux wakes this morning with a dream of mountains
        wind child with perfect breasts
                              glides lightly
in sheer robes   white teeth
                     her warm pets her
      wisdom plants
   I just have to move on
                     in floppy hats
    70 m.p.h.
              cruising turnpikes for
      sun bubbles . . .
                  pop open in mist
amazing grace
            up from cracked pavements
    more
          young girls in empty blouses
("You see through . . ."   they
      squat against fire
                 hydrants
with cupped hands inventing
        secrets that
            later you can't deny
   I watch
        little Jupiters whiz around my fingers
the space available to me
         from the place I sit
    to the place I dream

To a Poetess

You sit to have waves rush to your open hands
and you're surprised as cities grow there

        the cool air's
             driving flips

                      jammed with mini-spearguns

but this time they're real
facing you,
             with your private school stripes

Miss Hewitt's girls riding through the reservoir
                      (on horse(s)

the horizon goes limp   and finally
you're not so beautiful afterall

                  * * *

my arms shoot stiff   I justify a margin

            in that sense
            each vein glows

                  * * *

good   but what I really need

      a soft chair

            to nod on your boring rap
            I'd settle for a twelve year nap.

                * * *

you go on then:
I'll listen

       why either worry or hate or be confused . . .

because the sun's so available and

                    mostly for you

bikini doll

            I quit listening again   I even go

with one tiny spit   on your black lace toe

                        * * *

It's better here
with the polar bears   good

better   so   light dissolves and swells my blood
                          a process worth remembering

            instead   (it's noon)   I watch solar colors
                                          wash themselves on her skin

and She has nothing to do with you

                        * * *

six dozen wet beach umbrellas
the space between them

            fading and then dissolving America into "families":

I
don't
understand
any
of
this.

                    * * *

though You're worse than ever
better just make a date with never

                        with your bunches of radar fingers

you might as well dissever

                              (giant aspirins
                               in the sky)

relaxing the locked planets of this galaxy.

The Cosmopolitan Sense

An odyssey of error humbles the cosmopolitan
sense, Han's recurring heartache, his skipole
knifing a snowy bank on your pain,
and everything opens up like a racehorse
in a forest, something grows and the sidewalk lets go,
so faces move in from the rain throwing tools
and knives and questions, which, unanswered
close the covers of a book we insist on living in,
only there are roofs rising off the sidewalk
and small birds grab them in their beaks
to string them, these pearls, like beads or arrows
along the street that runs from here to Ferdinand's,
you know, the egoist with the split tongue.
To get there isn't easy under the roofs
fitted with dusty attics, perfect hideouts for books by moonlight
and tea by noon. Anything to clear the streets
of all those walkers, in fact anything to put near your ear
and cough by, anything to put in your pipe and smoke.
You see it doesn't matter if the rug comes out from under us,
because summer feels better in the desert in spite of the insects

who wish to nip our ears, but they are stopped
by a deadly spray under one roof, the spray of the sea,
as it rises to quench my thirst and it does
because I am innocent about death
and never wish to kill the idea
of a home, of a sad lonely night
when fiery ovals parachute out of the sky
picking up our heads so quickly the pipe
drops out of our mouth, and I reach to defend myself
knowing that forever I must stop the pain, the only purpose we're
    sure of
The rug comes out from under us
revealing fiery skies that think for themselves,
midnights overloaded with print, noon of the winds
knocking your window out over a bed, familiar as home

and the girder chained day, but you don't object
because it is the way of things to move in circles
partly because of color partly because of the great mountains
and trees thrown into it, like a pearl tossed
into a pod, the way some tiny gardener gets a thrill one day,
opening it up and becoming rich, thus a shiny **new tractor**
arrives and everyone sits down to watch.
We're all tiny gardeners in a sense, waiting for that tractor
and rehearsing without any clothes on as we move around and hope.
We re all things moved by color through mountains and into trees
thrilled by tiny gestures, a bright necktie, friendship, everything
tossing us: a frenzy, a blue, a giddy gulp.

written with Bruce Wolmer

Growing Up
for George Schneeman

we got lucky not too long ago
you showed up &
we improved
& we improved you too & that's true
but not too much
you've got the silver
and we've got the change
which proves something you tell us
that bodies have some interest
like feathers & trees and air too
and we agree with this
we think it's true
& we know you and we are better for it
so ante up George
the tension is incredible,
                    mounting

                    written with Ted Berrigan & Bill Berkson

Poem

The tea is boiling
sun in morning shade

my eyes squint on a red sofa
my teeth brushed electrically in the bath room
the rest of me does yoga on the lawn

your wife is turning pale, she is sick
of the hindu next door, sparkling lice
nest in her hair . . . I see

water flowers shoot up on thin layers of ocean fog

your son is in the corner tossing an epileptic fit . . .

we start to feel enclosed
like mannequins in storage start
to shiver, figure out someway to occupy our minds

start to knit or something

Cold Faces

1.
you breathe
through your mouth

saturate all things
on this resort beach

2.
the lightning moves closer
up the stairway
I watch the storm

To the Secret Poets of Kansas

Just because I can't understand you
it doesn't mean I hate you . . . like
when you go on continuously how you
cannot tolerate skyscrapers or cabdrivers

> maniac faces on Fifth, well

it means nothing to me I
just ignore as so often
or shift gears and read Pope or some
boring Russian lunatic . . . you can't deny future

> or simply fade.

and if you don't feel like running across streets here
you simply get run over and that means pain and boredom . . .
now isn't it amazing how you bring out logic in my poems.

I see nothing in a tree but lazy shade and nature
and that's not special, that's science

and all this concrete and steel and noise,
well, they've divided the simplest air to poems
some mornings, and we can't always rely on "Beauty" or gods

> you must learn

but so often on our losses . . . and our tears.

Jet Fizzle

It was summer then
and the forests were legal

the farmers there
use marble eggs as decoys

when those Hawks dive
they reach speeds up to 200 m.p.h.

disappointed

at egg

a switchman
a red lantern
in Grand Central Station

a jar of honey
in the plain brown bag

I thought
that it was pretty
weird

when he poured it in

God the fathers beard

Sea Battle

I fall out
crush the useless excess of god

my mouth most dry

each actor celebrates
his imminent "He must die"
shortage of great

like a chorus of nuns
every school morning . . . sing:

"child sang and child fell
and child rode right thru his shell
white plastic fish dissolve in that sea
I thank god for what has given me . . . "

SPECIAL WAVES
the sign reads

too many to see

the words say
"I be free,"
(I told her meant)
to change all eternity

so man lifts his head
forms his song
the land changes

as he murmurs

"It is as I said"

a president
or two

now and then found dead.

An Early Morning Crucifixion

Sands darkened by insects
and lights to measure the foggy distance,
we are going out there . . .   tonight
our pockets filled with the pressed blossom

                              across the giggling surf.

you had come here in secret and returned
and I barely saw the image against the warm grass,
it was more like a doctor or a soldier, because
to accept this breeze is to continue to choose, to distinguish.

                              you'll be quiet as that happens.

to see shadows on waves and the passion
tumble to the shore from this perfect edge,
to know the warmth of a hand placed diagonal
to the tree which a few minutes ago disappeared,

into a region where the cool stallion
tramples the night bather's wrist, and she
cries as if to warn the others to embrace,
bronze ladies running drenched along the gravel shores

Invisible Sleep

for Devereaux

Traces of pink Bergdorf light
dissolving into its furry air

nervously towed up
wrecked sidewalks

N.Y.C.'s bubble dawns
reminding me each year
of each year reversed

hazy puffed up sensibilities

                              I stole somewhere

shoot out . . .

snow trips snow
its clumsy grey fingers
like insects rolling somewhere beneath you

                         invisible sleep of winter

Hotel Plaza's elegant
stare through abandoned nostalgia zoos
                              phantom playgrounds
                              chained noise trucks
dragging down Fifth

just reflectingly plain and wet there.

music manages itself as usual everywhere
and I get lost lately if there's no packages to carry

lame fountains tempt lame birds
school girls fill buses to return someplace dreaming

and in the same room later on
I've been spacing my time
more often these days

                              the tiny notes of steam
releasing me, another year
in your thought out gaze.

Sure . . .

I got
a syringe

I use it
to baste
my tiny turkey

Fear and Trembling

To play Segovia
upon waking
is the highest I
might ever aspire to might
even shoot down the pain
dreams these hands
shake colorless they
can't forget and
in that way just can't defend

                              sun stirred
                                 in coffee
                                     by condensed air spoons

              and

on the bathroom floor on the porcelain there

                              blue blood

from the terrace the reservoir
evaporates in the violet tubes of
morning air, chokes miniature landscapes . . .
none of these processes fail me

                        only the flower

           too distant to imagine even . . .

though you sleep through . . .

           sunken eyes   radiate the bed

                        empties the frost
                            from the bars and windows

pouting torn   bending image

I watch the children you breathe dissolve
I see the plain girl the plain print gown

then I figured out what was real
blue blood

remember?   I noticed the morning and its sound

I noticed the scar
on your wrist as
the palms rise
to catch each tear

After St. John of the Cross

We humans
do not freeze often

but rather the dragon breathes
and our wrists are jolted from the fogs,

Sun, speak to me,
you are important.

no, that's not fire,
that's reason   which you might enjoy

                                        like a raisin

if the kitchen hadn't diminished
            before the trucks had arrived.

Mr. Hoffer,
            you are an enigma   I've decided
and earth
            you have flunked.

I am not impressed
by a cartoon character
who drives his hammer
against my thumb,

yet I goof
            on "a profound idea"

as I nod   in this century

        it squats in my hand   and licks,

folks,
            that isn't just any whistle
            that you happen to be hearing

it is a signal   it is 5 p.m.

now fold the ladder and
                           lay down the machete.

now run back through the rice paddy.

Little Ode on St. Anne's Day

You're growing up
and rain sort of remains
on the branches of a tree
that will someday rule the earth.

and that's good
that there's rain
it clears the month
of your sorry rainbow expressions

and clears the streets
of the silent armies . . .

so we can dance

Chop Chop

My pet creations fly away
I swat at pig air in the humid forest

I don't care for no bullshit, Mr. President,
I want thick quick cheeseburger

                                           chop chop

you merchants have no idea how great
it is to be here   (right here)

flipping bubblerings around the little girls
and jotting down their names on stones

                                         in the water

Prince, I hear the bed squeaking in the palace
because you and foxey are up to naughty naughty

it's great however
it's like being next to baby's breath

poor Spinoza!

he got excommunicated
because of some cosmic whim

and no one was allowed
within four cubits of him

Silver Mirrors

A horse moves
this weekend
into our living room

he says, "Oh, quickly
form a ring around me
as to prevent the merciless
insane hounds from attacking
my weakened legs in attempt
to drag me back to the icy
palace in the wintry regions."

"Then you are the one they sent?"

"yes"

"Very clever, did you bring it?"

"yes"

Highway Report

For Jack Kerouac

Breathe . . .
open fields
like tipping your hat to the sun

stream across turnpike

                                two women

on the other side   their dawns
reflect through the waters
on horses   tall weeds sensuous sway

crows settle

they assort their dreams

                            highway metal fences shine

three of us
feminine   marvelous   and tough

          our long hair
          rests on a cloud's eye
                              streaming

drinking codeine   and my body
at 70 m.p.h.   is feather

I raise a knife to the sky's neck
the sun curves to avoid me

(It didn't really curve)
the sun couldn't care less

                   good afternoon,
                   Mayakovsky

                                              my nod:
                                      a walk down St. Mark's Pl.

              with Ray Bremser

wearing a kimono . . .

Here comes the sun
over a.m. radio

                        nodded two hours

nation's capital ascends over
trees colored for my dream
along yr. highway life

Kerouac is dead at 47
                              on radio

and McCartney alive

              (we lost)   and

tragedy's just that and what to do but keep on going all in one line

                        * * *

        the joggers are jogging
        a president is lying

        (Last month my prick was "discharging")

                        let us pray

        Last highway trees and barns sway, the roads
        sighing wetly . . . clouds so low, they are filled
        with the snow of my heart, it's part of every man's
        dream to rise to the sky . . . to die, gone forever from
        American highways, where I nod today, missing nothing
        really . . . to disappear . . . at least for a time

        this clear October day.

Dog Crunch

The foot of
a dog
formed and crunched
a lake

as my ear
falls now

Love Poem (Later)

for Rise

The little bonus
of my hand on your breast
makes a bus seem so useful
when some rain begins to open.

then cloud waves cracked sun shafts
when the sky began to whistle
and I was thinking about it all night
just watching it move from my eye to my hand.

it's not very meaningless
the changes one makes lying down
it's almost the way a mountain feels
when it becomes a star

California Poem

The ocean fooled me
I thought it was bubble
but it was frozen spray
like a pain dream
and the double driftwood
and agates
surfers in rubber masks
and suits . . . like leather angels
leaning forward on their knees on
moon struck docks along Tenth Ave.
N.Y. . . . city of cowboy fantasies

and my own dreams beneath this blonde sun
of heroin and poolrooms childhood back home

you'll never return
yet you will go back
drawing more distinctions . . .
there, where my entire history
waits in sun puddles on filthy sidewalks
thousands of umbrellas poking my body

to wound the heart

and out here poets sleep beaches all day
with fears of Japan where bronze children
start landslides on their brains

Withdrawal Letter

Wild geese waking in the March wind

it's morning
I don't think much about March
though the weather disturbs me
and
the geese, they disappear eventually
with enormous groans of lost possibilities

I am truly a fragment of your secret worlds
though this eludes me. I think
all day about the likeness of heroin
to skindiving, how sharks never sleep
are marked from Southampton to Japan in three days

and how pure the waves are
no matter what the professors say,
in their motion . . . a gull glows in my sweat

                              Eastward

simple, yet the pain of remembering
so much before, so many gulls
seen and jammed into poems
this one just glided onto the reef
it was easy to include, and I trust it.

and horses, count the horses
in this poem and that
I saw a palomino once in Kansas and wept
the eye ring froze from each touch,
truck drivers passing on the highway
shouting with their fingers

though I nodded mostly through Kansas
treating someone I love badly, though
confusion results, and from there one realizes

it is not alone, anything
in the end, and one loves again
in this marvelous hollow decoration
each moves slowly within

you want to whisper, mainly of fear,
"Who are they?"

it is daylight now

the truth is you lost your willow
for me to find, for each muse to dance
why not joy to change pace
under these weeping leaves, only nature's gimmick

and "They," well, they surround you in N.Y.C.
on subways and park entrances near the plaza
but can you turn your head to the fountain?
I sit with my long hair breathing spray

and can I bear all those other scenes
so many other words might shoot up?

I want my hands and neck to be free and clear
no crucifixes and no rings.

these hands that hold the blood that rises
to a level where joy is pumped
visually to one's heart
in the serpent red dawn

Maybe I'm Amazed

Just because there is music
piped into the most false of revolutions

it cannot clean these senses
of slow wireless death crawling
from a slick mirror
1/8th it's normal size . . .

Marty was found dead by the man literally
blue 12 hours after falling out
at the foot of the Cloisters
with its millions in rare tapestry
and its clear view of the Hudson

and even testing your blue pills
over and over to reverse
my slow situations
I wind up stretched across the couch
still nodding with Sherlock Holmes
examining our crushed veins

Richard Brautigan,
I don't care who you are fucking
in your clean california air

I just don't care

though mine are more beautiful anyway
        (though more complex perhaps)

and we have white flowers too
right over our window on 10th St.
like hands that mark tiny x's
across infinity day by day

but even this crumb of life
I eventually surface toward

continues to nod as if I see you all
thoughtlessly
through a carefully inverted piece
of tainted glass

shattered in heaven
and found on these streets

Mercury Clouds

The waves pumping at you

                      like mercury clouds

    just a section of the universe showing off

closer than you imagine
sea birds are planning

                to divide a revolution

closer than that a mother
feeding her baby

                    (bright plaid beach chairs)

milk from the earth

           my body stands over.

New Year 1970

All the busted chairs out in the streets
getting iced no good for anyone anymore

all my footprints of the 60's across N.Y.C.'s sidewalks
gone, so important now I realize as if a head
was beaten in every inch of that zonked pathway

the 60's with its death of poetry
Frank O'Hara and Jack Kerouac
dead too in the pavement Olsen
dying quick moment now uptown
all last night without morphine
and why? "When it's hopeless,
give it to him, don't hesitate,"
I told Billy once, "no one works
it out on nerve when there's no nerve left."

and his is gone now, in the end

Charles Olsen

his long white hair in Gerard's photo
and my visions of Melville on looking

soon under pavement too, the rain-
soaked mattress against the stoop
shivering on 12th waiting for my man

"You better take that long pause about now . . ."

anyway everythings been driven away
and the heart has faded slightly like a tower

as you move

wasted presence
like a woods of ice
glaringly inhibited
for every new sign of the sun.

Midnight

The ambulance passes
we sit up

pinned eyes of nuns that genuflect between stars
ambassadors on marble staircases in steam tropics

and the cracked fingers of sculptured virgins
                                    reaching out . . .

I sit cross-legged on dead trees
that float like a saint's ghost I

watch genius natives grow insane by night
juggle fire out from their veins as babies

play astral chords on water stones, breathe
lovely notes lightly, make animals dream, I fade

Prell

Day changes from cannon to morning glory
her body dances death dances in the prell light

beads strung out all through Japan's public park's, my head,
light green eyes of the birds that break branches to build homes there.

she tore the page, "Varieties of Emeralds"
from little sister's picture encyclopedia.

I watched this all with a spike in my vein from a top floor window
I felt the blood pass from my arm into the glass tube above it . . .

then it was rainy bonzais everywhere for me
and black masses across my brain like planets on solar maps

paper secrets I used to believe lined the open closet shelves
her body split and floated into the air forests like astral monkeys.

It's there, the air the body the soft green day:
your life cutting through the light noise of New York City's traffic
    dawn.

Back Home

Sick morning . . . school kids
playing soccer in the past
thin shaftways of graceful nostalgia
touch down my brain
sky nails falling . . .
seals silver coffin
at last and
I am happy and breathing sweat as
coils of pinkish heat make my brain sleepy I sail

over your bubble cities and watch
with secret eyes the money stomping and
great buildings rise like an empty syringe
filling with the glassy blood one thousand . . .
secretaries and vice presidents on and on
wasted energy beings with hearts
that dream of their lover's spit . . .
compressed nights in bars and toolshops
complex as a pill

as I drift
like the tongues of your patron saints
through liquid planets and ghost stars
abandoned by the children, back home . . .

who signal now to greet me
before I was born

For Sue's Birthday

There is a wind on 91st St. all night

      (very simple wind)

it simply blows up here
to apt. 10S

  opens our windows
shakes my nose

    and says, "wake up, idiot, wake up,"

And now I've woken up.

(hello little moth,
  landing on the yellow primrose
  there on the corner table,

  stay here all winter if you like

  stay warm,

  so when summer comes
  you can get back in the open again

   fly a little above the hassles
      so to speak,

  touch someone else now and then

      (simple idea)

and can we join you,
    little moth,
  will you wait for us?

Down from the ceiling flies a heart
    which gracefully lands on my sleeve:

and now we are young again
returning home at lunchtime
three of us
beginning everyday
to breathe the mystery
which has somehow lead us "here"

how did we get "here"?
                    what happened?

we're in a giant meadow now
our legs crossed on a sofa
we shiver from the week-old snow
which leans against our thighs
as a flower would rest beside a watermill

    which is overflowing with some incredible joy
                                    onto our eyes.

Sue, I think I'll just stare at it awhile
        because out there the reservoir is so filled
        and morning touches over it like a dancer:
                                    yellow and naked and wet.

    and Sue
            I think you should know
            that two people who love you so very much
            are caring for you an awful lot lately

    especially on the day that you were born:

                                    which is simply today.

which is why I'm writing this poem,
                    —especially for you.

Song

In minute gestures
                that jet wetly slight
      right above your eyes
                                    each morning
I watch the sun cross over the reservoir
                all day sometimes
                        a few hours soaked into air cotton
like cloud syringes drawing up blue
                                like darkness when it's through

Poem

This country invades me

and you can join me

                   if you know . . .

I feel   an uneasy warmth
blue mist of grass fingers   gliding thru my pulse
that clear abandoned infants
from the day's movements

                 their strange eyes

rushes of pure summer
that later form energy tulips

they polish eyes
in light ballets
            that hum

I begin
     to sing
         to its sway

the warmth   shoots
                  light missiles
                     of blue oxygen

thru my lungs
         you know . . .

those babies breathe
too heavy

                     strange eyes

air that shatters into sweet inspiration

Love Story

The penalty for desertion
is death by a firing squad.

I'm saving you this trouble

enclosed is a pistol.
loaded with only one bullet.
squeeze the trigger once
perhaps nothing will happen.

but squeeze a second time . . .
a third time . . .   You see

I know the games you love

In This Room Particularly

I wake to move easy

                    (a sacred heart
                    carved in wood
                    rests over my shoulder)

with a sense that

through this Japanese garden

                    (my head)

laced with plums falling
noiseless and unbruised

                       in my head

you see

          you're the one . . .

will be stuck
among those branches

        I created

              up there

too strong

for a long time to pass

thru the river in your view in my head

The Tenth Try

I owe a lot to someone
I've watched her tear
fall like an icarus
it was like a star
which is the sun
who is me.

it won't be long
that I will look up
and feel the sounds again
that I pretend sometimes
that they are gone forever.

the steps are simple
to walk in this universe
you must feel each one distinct
as if someone had died
their faces designating each constellation.

you realize
what connects that time you spent
lying on the lawn you remember
is not so long before
and, say, the beauty of the statue
you saw last monday an angel there
her lips hung over the garden, the stone garden.

that connection
is not so easy finding it
in one's mind
and yet the solution
is but a clue . . . the garden, the stone garden . . .
to all you have meant to me
and why this is so.

Love Poem

for Cassy

I see myself, sad now, as in a mirror
appearing before us sad now as in a movie that lies.

I am sick of N.Y.C. but I hate
adobe huts and sad communes
with naked girls carrying hunting knives
nailed to their sides 10,000 ft. above Manhattan.

so I walk
down gloomy Park Ave South early morning
in my head one more time
with its dawn churches
with their stained glass dripping
like your eyes I see
before me in a mirror
waking slowly in daylight.

For Your Birthday

for D.C.

It is right
to be exactly the way it is
where even the sun won't begin
runs fast away
birds gather specks of white petals
and leave them in circles for the nuns to watch
when they pass the window to greet/ the paths
this morning

> and that happens every day this time

let me tell you
that I have survived all
I have seen through windows . . .
I formed no ideas except that one . . .
that one like the story of the man and hunter
that night shaking hands in the wintry inn
was he leaving or had he just arrived?

> night surrounded by star streams like gauze.

and I've avoided
the image that my heart
might some other time recall
although at times the wind advances into the nest
which hides the metals and cakes they have all presented me

what I wanted
was a narrow room
filled with simple love and exact emotions
no symbols and no dreams
one notion two might survive forever
though we will not always believe it, after all,

the rain gathers the stones always

and in winter
the stones are eyes

their dim freeze holding

Poem

Yesterday you past
into your lips . . . your hips
and your breasts
a poor unconsummated memory

we spent sick days
was tragic sometimes
sometimes was silly

but sometimes it was on a sweet log
on a long walk after dinner
in your windy warm energy jeans

fingers touching.

On the Rush

I stuck out my palm . . .
the snow the pine needles
hit lightly

I thought it was rain for a minute
I thought the game had been called

Words from Babylon

Africa is bleeding
from the rape of her light

all black men are thus
those who are ambivalent toward her

here in Babylon
our hands revolutionize
and make green
love

and then?

and then?

Torn Canvas

A man passes through a gate
as wide as his eyes

his wife stands before it thirteen hours
she waits

she cries

The Birth and Death of the Sun

Now the trees tempt
the young girl below them

each moves off the other's wind
endlessly, as stars from the earth,

stars from the stars.

It Doesn't Matter

Though the phonograph got melted and the radio
is angry sounds, yawning mammal stampedes at dawn

sounds . . . you know? because I'm far down in the insect
sweat where underfed boney cherubs clog my ears . . .

whisper over our fates . . . their's: leukemia . . . mine: poetry
its possibilities . . . like the young girl signaling

at the water's edge, gate to music cool as green insect
wings rise up from down's sweaty pools; my eyes

jackhammer through the fog up to clear space, walk out
to the watery gate, music fixed up in surf, ends the poem . . .

seals my fate.

Chelsea May

A pair of frozen dice come
tumble through picture windows
the sun slips out and
she is standing at the gate
with all her possibilities

I conceal so much
moving in and out poetry
I could have simply left a note
tell you how I hate
getting up each morning and
drink coffee, feel unslightly sick and . . .

What Coleridge couldn't admit, well,
DeQuincey, he cashed in on it.

do you see,
                    Chelsea May?

it's just a feeling I have at times
I want to live until I want to die
and I don't want their cures
no matter what I say
my mind is shot into storms
and she's leaning on the gate etc. . . .

Savage Bubbles

for Carol Kane

You shift
into lonely music
trail fading emeralds and cocaine leopards

          * * *

I snag you raw
at snake games in white rooms
smashed windows
like babies afraid of colors

          * * *

These leopards are animal proud
sexy quick   astral masters
of jungle nights, frozen
dramas in the camera's eye,
blink . . . ocean rush . . . dawn rests on us
the pads of your eyes

          * * *

Sleep
to sleep
to sleep inside insect ballets
to sleep in landscapes
on painted doors, icy windows

          * * *

Great morning of Plan Zoo
we gather to break bars
crush cages, dawn streaked
like the mandrill's stare, we free
eaters of meat to the city plazas

          * * *

I fade
into your vibes

we skate Fifth Ave.
on its frozen fear

    (You can make suns rise
       Incredible brain surf!

    It happens!
              Savage bubbles)

      * * *

Breathe still
huddled dreams for softness
kitten bellies flow
ear to ear
where long hair lay

      * * *

That's another
city dream on waking with
your gypsy eyes
uncombed with
your ankles raised
like flags

Paregoric Babies

Clocks blue seconds fold over me
slow as swamp dreams I feel
heavy like metal shade pre-dawn thickness

                                    I sit

in my chair of nods shivering
from a sickness I took years to perfect

dark paddling in the wave membrane
the monkey woman's dream streams
are places of shy creatures, head infants
I had born on a whim and abandoned . . . my eye

drips the strain in the sweet March air, frozen
pure as my blood refuses to flow . . .
stilled, sweat that shines the breath of my poem

An Apple at Dawn

The orange in side walk

                          is shivering
is morning   light
      near the park   a tree
opening up   sparkling breakfasts

        a couple of million

moving people   moving along
into the grace of victories

                              in the air
                              a finger

in the water   a face
        your own
and others   a french schoolgirl
      for one   humming on a bus

              a breeze assembled

in your fist   a voice rehearsing
in your lap   because lately "you get"

            (the wing lift mildly:
                      they're COLD AND ENDURING
your body is pumping:
                      it is filled with blood.

you don't really feel totally useless,

                  do you?

        and you're occasionally aware.

. . . these stringy clouds   look out Manhattan

            your prince's sorrow

      might be back   again   tomorrow.

FOR THE BEST IN PAPERBACKS, LOOK FOR THE

In every corner of the world, on every subject under the sun, Penguin represents quality and variety—the very best in publishing today.

For complete information about books available from Penguin—including Pelicans, Puffins, Peregrines, and Penguin Classics—and how to order them, write to us at the appropriate address below. Please note that for copyright reasons the selection of books varies from country to country.

In the United Kingdom: For a complete list of books available from Penguin in the U.K., please write to *Dept E.P., Penguin Books Ltd, Harmondsworth, Middlesex, UB7 0DA*.

In the United States: For a complete list of books available from Penguin in the U.S., please write to *Consumer Sales, Penguin USA, P.O. Box 999— Dept. 17109, Bergenfield, New Jersey 07621-0120*. VISA and MasterCard holders call 1-800-253-6476 to order all Penguin titles.

In Canada: For a complete list of books available from Penguin in Canada, please write to *Penguin Books Canada Ltd, 10 Alcorn Avenue, Suite 300, Toronto, Ontario, Canada M4V 3B2*.

In Australia: For a complete list of books available from Penguin in Australia, please write to the *Marketing Department, Penguin Books Ltd, P.O. Box 257, Ringwood, Victoria 3134*.

In New Zealand: For a complete list of books available from Penguin in New Zealand, please write to the *Marketing Department, Penguin Books (NZ) Ltd, Private Bag, Takapuna, Auckland 9*.

In India: For a complete list of books available from Penguin, please write to *Penguin Overseas Ltd, 706 Eros Apartments, 56 Nehru Place, New Delhi, 110019*.

In Holland: For a complete list of books available from Penguin in Holland, please write to *Penguin Books Nederland B.V., Postbus 195, NL-1380AD Weesp, Netherlands*.

In Germany: For a complete list of books available from Penguin, please write to *Penguin Books Ltd, Friedrichstrasse 10-12, D-6000 Frankfurt Main I, Federal Republic of Germany*.

In Spain: For a complete list of books available from Penguin in Spain, please write to *Longman, Penguin España, Calle San Nicolas 15, E-28013 Madrid, Spain*.

In Japan: For a complete list of books available from Penguin in Japan, please write to *Longman Penguin Japan Co Ltd, Yamaguchi Building, 2-12-9 Kanda Jimbocho, Chiyoda-Ku, Tokyo 101, Japan*.